A kid's BESTIARY OF ANCIENT NUBIA

ISAC MUSEUM

the Wildlife of Ancient Nubia

Hello, my name is *Zaraafa,* which means "giraffe" in Arabic.

A **bestiary** is a book with stories about different animals, both real and imaginary, and I'm going to tell you about the animals found in ancient Nubia, where my **ancestors** came from. I now live in southern Sudan because climate change made it impossible to live in Nubia.

Nubia is a region in North Africa located along the Nile River between southern Egypt and northern Sudan. If you look at the map, the Nile flows through the country from south to north. For thousands of years, the river, and the **fertile** land on either side, was home to hundreds of different animals both large and small.

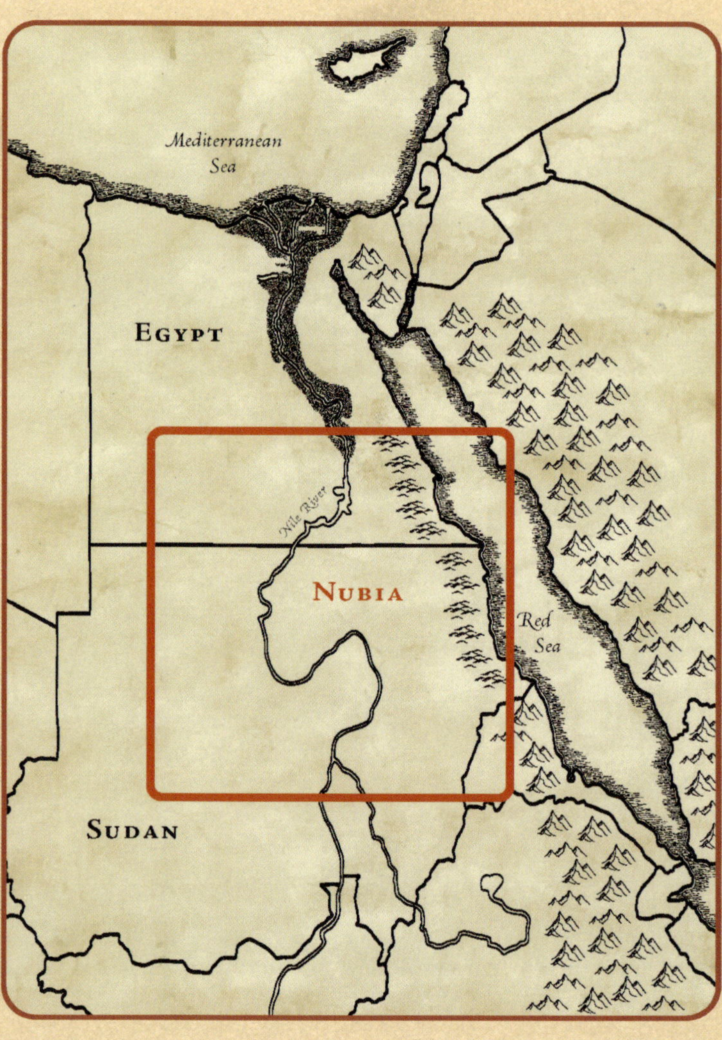

Handy hint:
If you see a word in **bold**, you can look up its meaning in the glossary at the back of this book.

About 6,000 years ago...

Nubia underwent a major **transformation**. The climate began to change, and less rainfall led to a **decline** in tropical trees and vegetation, turning rich pastures into desert. The landscape changed forever. This had a major effect on the wildlife that lived there. Humans and animals moved closer to the river, and large **herbivores** such as elephants, and my distant relatives, moved south in search of water and food.

At the same time...

the development of farming increased competition for food between the **domestic** and wild animals that lived along the river. Some animals, like antelope, disappeared from the **savanna** because of cattle herds. Today, only a small number of mammals, reptiles, and insects live in Nubia.

This picture shows graffiti of elephants and giraffes on rocks at a place called El-Egeba. Dr. James Henry Breasted, who founded ISAC, took this picture in 1906. He wrote in his diary "that these animals had been **extinct** in Nubia for some 5,000 years and the carvings must be at least as old as that time". It is hard to see, so archaeologists traced the animals and you can see their outlines on the left.

A Q E J A J L T H D G I R A F F E S S L C W
D E S S B O S E M O S Q U I T O E S N B N J
O L T H I P H Q A E T T V G L R S M K Y O R
R T O E H L C K I U H P Y O H C L V W F O M
Y T R E B V P L B C N P R D A A A W A T B O
S A K P Q I F E R V J M Q A P I R T H E A N
U C G E E S E E G X W H G H R T K E F J B K
M N N K C W P B I E Y X W O J V Y N O I J E
A R L I A E Z Y P M T E N W A O E O E S S Y
T O L I L V N C M N L O E X H T S G L W T H
O H X I E G D V B T I F L X L M S E E C M V
P G N X M R W F E L C T I N K A B S P F L F
O N M C Q T K E L C F F D I D R L A H I L X
P O X S Y P B A N T E L O P E L R F A S D B
P L X C K B D Z I L D B C T S B V J N I A D
I M F O A R C J X N S E O A O K I K T B G N
H B J R A R O H A E Y E R C U R S T X I X O
X C A P I M R O P R R S C P C H E E T A H C
N C O I M W Q R V U L T U R E C E Y A Y V L
S E K O L C D S D U C K T H F I N C H P C A
L B K N K Z L E W A R T H O G A C K Z V S F
S M D K J T K E S J G Z J Q S K J O Z U Q Z

Can you find these animals that used to live in ancient Nubia?

Hint: the words can be found in all directions.

Antelope	Dog	Giraffe	Lark	Pig
Baboon	Duck	Goat	Leopard	Scarab beetle
Bees	Elephant	Hare	Lion	Scorpion
Catfish	Falcon	Hawk	Longhorn cattle	Sheep
Cheetah	Finch	Hippopotamus	Monkey	Stork
Cobra	Flies	Horse	Mosquitoes	Vulture
Crocodile	Geese	Ibis	Nile perch	Warthog

Animals in Archaeology

We know about the animals that once lived in Nubia from **archaeological excavations**. Animals are depicted on things like pottery, rock art, and jewelry. We also find objects made from animal products such as bone, leather, and shell, as well as objects used to hunt and fish including arrowheads, fishhooks, and nets. Just like today, animals were reared for food, hunted, and kept as pets. The picture below shows a bell worn by camels.

Some animals you might expect to see in ancient Nubia, such as crocodiles, falcons, and snakes, but others you might be surprised by, including elephants, hares, and even monkeys. We know there were giraffes not only because of the picture taken of the rock art, but images of my ancestors also appear on paintings, pottery, and other objects such as the ostrich eggshell below.

Can you see the giraffe etched on this piece of ostrich eggshell?

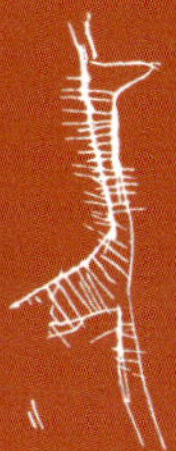

Here are some objects from our collection that show us what animals once lived in ancient Nubia.

Our curator mixed up the labels when putting them on display.
Can you draw lines to match the object with the correct label?

1

2

3

4

5

6

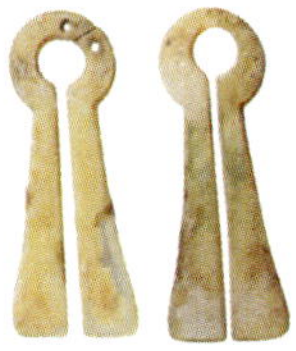

A Leather quiver with crocodile image found in a grave.
About 1,600 years old.

B Limestone incense burner with large feline.
About 5,000 years old.

C Pottery jar with animal procession, including guinea fowl and hare.
About 2,000 years old.

D Keyhole-shaped hairpins made of shell.
One shows signs of repair in ancient times.
About 4,000 years old.

E Baked-clay statue of a hippopotamus.
These animals represented the enemies of the ruler.
About 5,000 years old.

F Ivory bracelet found in a tomb.
About 4,000 years old.

Animal Jumble! All of these animals have been traced from original images found on ancient Nubian objects or in paintings. How many different animals can you count? Hint: one animal appears twice—can you spot which one it is? Do you think you could name the different animals?

Living with Animals Real...

Animals were important to ancient Nubian **economy** and **culture**. Nubians herded animals such as cattle, goats, and sheep. Cattle were central to agriculture and used for plowing and pulling things. Along with goats and sheep, they were also kept for their milk, meat, and hides.

Fish and birds provided a good source of food and were roasted, dried, and salted, while bees were kept for honey and wax. Nubians kept dogs and even monkeys as pets. Pictures show dogs wearing collars and on leashes, and monkeys monkeying around. This picture from an Egyptian tomb shows a monkey climbing the neck of a giraffe in Nubia.

Dogs, like the saluki, were also used for hunting. Elephants and hippopotami were hunted for the ivory from their teeth and tusks; antelope for their meat, hides, and horns; and cheetahs and leopards for their pelts. Images, like the one below, show men wearing these pelts around their waists. You can also see animals, including a giraffe, being given as gifts to the Egyptian pharaoh.

Nubians were skilled **archers** who fought on horseback. Some were hired as paid soldiers. This saddle is made of leather and is 2,000 years old. It was found in a burial at Qustul. You can see it, along with a quiver (shown on a previous page), on display in our Nubian gallery. The image on the left shows a 16th century drawing of a Nubian archer.

... and Imaginary

Religion...

played an important part in the lives of ancient Nubians. Parts of ancient Egyptian **iconography** were borrowed and then changed to suit the Nubians' needs. For example, both cultures revered falcons, hawks, and vultures.

These pictures on the Narmer Palette and the Two Dog Palette show a serpopard. This mythical creature is a cross between a snake and a leopard. Some have the body of a snake and the head and neck of a leopard, while others are the opposite. People think this was really a picture of a giraffe drawn by someone who had never seen one. Even when Nubians had seen giraffes, the serpopard remained a mythical creature that offered protection and power.

Falcons & hawks...

represented the Egyptian god Horus, who had a falcon head and was the symbol of kingship and divine power. Nubian gods and rulers wore falcon-headed crowns or were shown with falcons above their heads.

Vultures...

were associated with royal protection and motherhood. The vulture-headed Egyptian goddess Nekhbet protected Upper Egypt and influenced the clothes worn by Nubian goddesses and queens.

Mythical beasts were common in Nubian religion. As well as the different animal-headed gods, there were also other fantastical creatures such as winged giraffes, ram-headed cobras, and lion-headed bees. This photo shows a lion-headed snake on a temple at a place called Naga.

Why not try creating your own mythical beast?
You can try combining different parts of your favorite animals!

Did you know...

both Nubians and Egyptians believed in the *ba*-bird. This creature had the head of a human and the body of a bird. The *ba* was the personality part of a person's soul. The *ba* could cross between the worlds of the living and the dead. Every day it could leave the tomb and fly around to visit friends, and every night it would return to the body in its tomb. You can see this statue in our Nubian gallery. It is about 1,700 years old.

Ba-bird Challenge!

The *ba*-bird is trying to find its way back to the tomb. Can you help it?

Answers

Matching: 1F, 2E, 3A, 4B, 5C, 6D

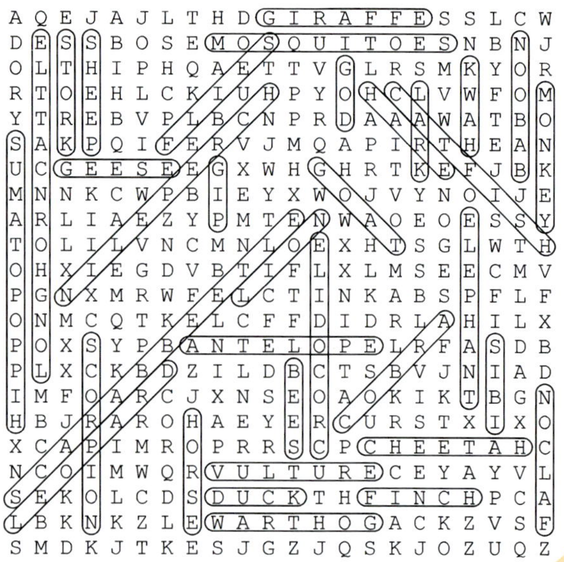

Animal Jumble: There are 37 animals in total, and 2 scarab beetles.

Image credits:

1. Valerian Guillot from Cambridge, United Kingdom
2. Ray in Manila, African Bush Elephants, Amboseli National Park & BN Chagny – Aerial View of the Nubian pyramids at Meroe. Image owner Francis Geius Mission SFDAS 2001
6. LeGabrie, Nubian Archer, Codex Casanatense
7. Nina R, Sudan, Nubian Pyramids
8. Nina R, Sudan, Nubian Pyramids
9. Nina R, Sudan, Nubian Pyramids

Bonus challenge: Can you find all the tiny frogs hiding inside this book ? There are 7 of them!

Glossary

Ancestors
An ancestor is someone you are related to. Ancestors are usually older than your grandparents.

Archaeological Excavations
People who study the past through the things people left behind are called archaeologists. Archaeological excavations are where archaeologists dig up the ground to discover these things (artifacts), which can range from tiny items of jewelry, pottery, and tools to large buildings. Archaeologists also study skeletons of animals and humans.

Archer
People who use a bow and arrow, like Robin Hood or Katniss from the Hunger Games.

Bestiary
A collection of stories or descriptions about animals both real and imaginary.

Culture
Things that a group of people have in common like language, food, or clothes that make them unique.

Decline
A change to a lower level, such as a decrease in the population of an endangered animal.

Domestic
This is something that is related to things that happen at home with your family like tidying your bedroom. A domestic animal would be a pet that lives with you or that you look after like farm animals. Domestic can also mean within a country such as domestic travel from one part of the country to another.

Economy
The way people make money and then spend it. In the past when there was no money, people would trade things instead, such as wool to turn into cloth for grain to turn into food.

Extinct
The last plant or animal of its kind is no longer alive. For example, the West African black rhino went extinct due to hunters illegally killing it for its horn.

Fertile
Good for growing crops or producing offspring.

Herbivore
An animal that eats only plants and does not eat meat.

Iconography
A symbol or image that tells a story without using words a bit like emojis.

Revered
Something or someone that is thought of very highly, like a president, a king or queen, a god, or even your favorite celebrity (like Mr. Beast).

Savanna
A type of flat, grassy landscape with scattered trees spread across a wide area. Savannas are usually found in tropical or subtropical regions.

Transformation
A major change that happens to something, like a caterpillar turning into a butterfly.

THE UNIVERSITY OF CHICAGO
INSTITUTE FOR THE STUDY OF ANCIENT CULTURES MUSEUM
West Asia & North Africa

1155 E. 58th St.
Chicago, IL 60637
isac.uchicago.edu

For visitor information and museum hours:
isac.uchicago.edu/visit-museum

9 781614 911548 >